ALSO BY THOMAS CHRISTOPHER GREENE

Mirror Lake (2003)
I'll Never Be Long Gone (2005)
Envious Moon (2007)
The Headmaster's Wife (2014)
If I Forget You (2016)
The Perfect Liar (2019)

Notes from the Porch

Notes from the Porch

Tiny True Stories to Make You Feel Better about the World

Thomas Christopher Greene

Rootstock Publishing
Montpelier, VT

Notes from the Porch copyright ©2024 Thomas Christopher Greene

Release Date: February 20, 2024

Printed in the USA.

Published by Rootstock Publishing,
an imprint of Ziggy Media LLC
Montpelier, Vermont
info@rootstockpublishing.com
www.rootstockpublishing.com

Hardcover ISBN: 978-1-57869-160-9
eBook ISBN: 978-1-57869-161-6

Library of Congress Control Number: 2023947952

Cover and book design by Eddie Vincent, ENC Graphics Services.

For permissions, or to schedule a reading, contact the author at thomas.greene@vcfa.edu.

For my Mom

Author's Note

I was very fortunate and privileged during the worst of the pandemic. I was in the safest state in the country, and I didn't have to work outside the home. I spent my time in my old Victorian in downtown Montpelier, Vermont, and at my cabin on a lake north of here.

Before Covid-19, I wasn't home a lot. I was out all the time, telling stories, listening to stories, in restaurants every single night. A novelist, a college president, and a relentlessly social extrovert. Suddenly, I was alone. My daughter and her mother live a block away, and I saw them every single day for a few hours. But otherwise, it was just me, on my front porch in good weather.

They say a good Irishman should be able to get a story out of a trip to the post office. Covid-19 stole so much. But one of the things it couldn't steal was the power of stories. It turns out that stories sometimes find us. They are all around us if we are open to them, if we believe in magic, if we listen, and if we invite them into our lives.

The short vignettes that follow are all ones I told on social media during the pandemic as a way to feel less alone. The response they got suggested to me that maybe more people should hear them. I hope they make you laugh, smile, wonder, and bring you a measure of joy.

Neglected Gardens

A fall day and I was on my porch writing when a woman in her late sixties came down the street, saw me there, walked over and introduced herself. She used to live in my house. I didn't buy it from her—there was a couple here for three years in between. I've owned this place for four and a half years now. She and her husband had lived here for twenty-eight years. The house came with incredible elaborate gardens, which as I discovered talking with her were her life's work. I don't garden. In fact, I barely see plants. I spend too much time in my head, I told her. I've hired people to help me with them off and on in the time I've been here, but no one with enough focus and time to fully bring them back.

She said, well, that's why I'm here. This is going to sound weird, she said. But your neighbors tell me you're a laid-back guy. Would you mind if I worked in these gardens again? I'll stay out of your hair. It gives me peace, she said. We live in a condo now. A half mile away. The only thing I miss is the gardening.

That would be amazing, I said.

You sure?

Absolutely.

It's not weird?

It's only weird if we make it weird, right?

The weather the next bunch of days was a gift. Unseasonably warm for this time of year. I was able to write again on my porch. And all day long, from early morning till dusk, she was out there, eight feet away or so, tearing apart these beds, planting new things, designed for next spring. At times we told stories about our lives but mostly we worked. She would ask me to look at things and say, I'm thinking of doing this....

And I finally said, you know what? Consider this your canvas. You're an artist. Do what you would have done if you still lived here.

She smiled broadly at this. Okay, thank you, you sure it isn't weird?

No, it's amazing.

And the best part was all day long people stopped by to say hello to her, neighbors who remembered when she lived here. There was the moment before they saw me where you knew they thought she had lost her mind. Maybe someone should be called since she hasn't lived here in a long time? Nah. Just new friends making art together.

Neighborhood Boy #1

W ith the change in the weather, I've been writing on my front porch for the last week or so. I sit out with my laptop and tea, and my novel and I watch the neighborhood move past. There's this one neighborhood kid I admire. He's seven. The reason I know that is because he told me. He stopped on his bike in front of my porch and said, hey, Tom, guess what?

I said, what?

He said, I'm seven.

I said, this just happen?

Yesterday.

Happy birthday, buddy.

Thanks, man, he said.

That's what he said. Thanks, man.

But the reason I admire him is not that he's seven. It's how awesome he is on a bike–seriously, he's elite. He jumps over curbs.

He does wheelies. He goes ripping down the streets with no hands. He stops on a dime. Sometimes he's on a scooter or a skateboard. He does jumps. He's reckless. If he's by himself, he rides hard. If he's with a friend, sometimes they play pretend games, occasionally with squirt guns. I see him in the morning. I see him in the afternoon, and I see him at night. He's always outside. Maybe he's on a phone or video game other times but it can't be much. He's like a 1970s kid, though he wears a helmet. He reminds me of me, of my brothers, of a youth when we were free range, when my mother literally rang a distant bell to tell us to get home, not a buzz on a phone in our pocket.

The other night a wild storm came through town. I knew my own fourteen-year-old was out with her friends. I wrote her mom and she texted me back and said, I'm picking her up. Phew, I thought. I was on my porch. The rain was torrential and sideways. I looked out and this kid ran by, barefoot, t-shirt and jeans on, and I yelled at him, you're crazy!

He stopped. The rain matted his hair. It was dumping. He said, my mother told me to. And then he laughed with his head to the sky and let it wash over him.

Cinderella

A couple of years ago I was on a book tour. Book tours, at least for me, tend not to be glamorous affairs. My first night I read in a mall bookstore near Providence, Rhode Island. Four people were there, one of which was my young recent college grad niece. The only book sold was the one I bought for her. I slept in a Holiday Inn next to the airport and all night I listened to jets taking off and landing.

The following night I was reading in Westerly, Rhode Island, down by the coast, and my assistant had booked me a room at some nearby inn. I took my time driving there. It was February and so there was no traffic on the coast. It was a surprisingly seasonal day, though, no snow anywhere, and temperatures in the high forties. After a little bit of trouble, my navigation system led me to the inn where I was staying. It was a gorgeous spot, on a cliff looking out at Narragansett Bay. Beautiful old place that must be incredible in the summer. When I pulled into the sandy parking lot, I was the only car. No sooner had I parked, then an earnest young bellboy was next to my window. When I stepped out, he said, Mr. Greene?

Yes.

We've been expecting you. Can I get your bags?

Sure, I said.

I opened the back and gave him my suitcase. The two of us walked toward the front door. When we got there, and opened it, it was like when the Queen of England returned to Windsor Castle.

There was a staircase leading up to the lobby, and lining it, on both sides, was everyone who worked at the hotel. A gauntlet of waiters and bellboys and maids and chefs in their whites and their toques. I had never seen anything like it. As I walked through them, they said to me, Mr. Greene, welcome, sir. Welcome, Mr. Greene. Thank you, I said. Over and over.

At the front desk, the gentleman said to me, Mr. Greene, we understand you like champagne. We have for you today a perfectly chilled bottle of Veuve Clicquot. Might we pour you a glass while you check in?

You might, I said.

What follows is a great show around it, a brief presentation of the bottle, followed by a young waiter popping it into a towel then pouring it in a flute before handing it to me.

Mr. Greene, the gentleman said. We have upgraded you to the Ocean suite. We hope you enjoy your stay.

This place is great, I said.

Well, thank you, sir.

They bring me up to this extraordinary room, banks of windows on both sides. One that looks out to the wide Atlantic Ocean. The other, to a tidal river. Huge clawfoot tub elevated on the ocean side. On a desk, in elaborate calligraphy, are directions to the bookstore and back. I had been in the room for five minutes when there was a knock on the door. A woman was standing there with a large piece of slate. On it were elaborately crafted desserts, one an edible gold nest filled with tiny chocolates.

The chef understands you like sweets, she said.

I do indeed, I said.

That afternoon I walked around the extraordinary grounds, checked out the ocean views. Everywhere I went, staff greeted me. Looking good, Mr. Greene!

Feeling good, Jimmy! I called back.

The pièce de résistance though was the call I got from the front desk a little before five. We have for you, Mr. Greene, to drive to your reading, a brand-new BMW 740, if you're interested. We can provide you with a driver or if you'd like you can drive it yourself....

I'll drive it, I said.

I went to the reading. Great crowd. Probably fifty people. I read and answered questions, signed books. The car was insane. Hugged the coastline. I pushed it more than I should, but most likely I would never drive a car like this again.

When I got back to the hotel, I asked at the front desk, is the restaurant still serving dinner?

Oh, yes, they're expecting you, he said.

I was the only one in the restaurant. They had already decided what they would serve me. No menu. There were local oysters, then a buttered poached lobster and sea bass, and then a molten chocolate cake. A beautiful bottle of white burgundy.

Halfway through dinner, a very dapper older man came down the stairs to the restaurant. He came over to me and said, in a clipped British accent, you must be Mr. Greene.

I am.

He was the owner. He saw the copy of my novel, *The Perfect Liar*, next to me. He picked it up. Is this the book?

It was.

Story of my ex-wife, he said, and he laughed loudly at this. I confess I haven't read any of your books. She's a huge fan though. I have seen some of the movies though.

Movies? I said, imagining suddenly an alternate universe where my books were movies.

Yeah, there's the one with Matthew McConaughey and that one with Matt Damon where he's with the sick kid? Oh, yeah and Tom Cruise. *The Firm*, that one.

That's John Grisham, I said. He wrote those books.

Oh, that's not you?

No, it's not me.

The next morning, I slept late. I came downstairs and asked the front desk if they were still serving breakfast. The guy who the day before had opened me a bottle of champagne was reading the newspaper and barely looked up at me when I spoke. He looked down at his watch and said, oh, sorry, just missed it. There's a Dunkin' Donuts out by the highway, though.

Regret

The night before the pandemic, we slow-danced in my kitchen after midnight. We danced to a song we both loved, and as soon as it ended, I would press the button on my phone to make it play again. Okay, I'll tell you what it was. It was a song called "Lost in the Light." Her voice was beautiful, almost as beautiful as she was, and she sang the words to me as we danced.

It's funny the things you take for granted: her breath, my breath, my hands on the small of her back, moving up to push her long brown hair out of the way so I could see the part of her I loved the most, her face. Those sad milk chocolate eyes, slightly upturned nose, her lovely brown skin. We danced for hours. She sang. Somewhere our bodies met, curved into each other like stars. If only I had known, if only I had known, if only I had known I would never see her again, you see what I am saying?

I wouldn't have let that night end. I wouldn't have gone to sleep. The morning sun would have rudely been the one to tell us it was a new day and that it was over.

Mirror Lake

In 1993, my college girlfriend and I moved to Vermont. We lived in Montpelier for a month before we moved to a tiny cabin on a hill in Calais that had a wood stove in the basement as its only heat and no staircases, only ladders to the basement and up to the one bedroom. We were cold all the time, but we could see Camel's Hump and all the foothills leading up to it and we were young and in love and sometimes that's all that matters.

A couple of years later, we rented a second house, this small red farmhouse in a little valley and from which you couldn't see any other houses. We had been there for a while when someone told us that Clyde Dailey might want to sell his old farmhouse overlooking Mirror Lake, better known to the locals as Number 10 pond. I was twenty-seven years old, broke and with shitty credit. But I went to visit Clyde, whom I had never met, and who was ninety-six years old. Stepping into that house to talk to him was like stepping back in time. He was a hoarder, and the house was full of things stacked everywhere. It was winter. He had a fire going and he sat in front of it surrounded by boxes and stacks of paper and things in plastic bags. He wore three coats rather than use the oil heat. The house was crazy rundown, but you could tell it had good bones, but also something else, a feeling. Good juju. Every window looked down at the placid expense of lake below. I told him I wanted to buy his house, but that I didn't have a lot of money. We talked for a while, and he said he would think about it. I got a call from a lawyer about a week later. Clyde wanted me to buy the house and the forty acres of land, a mix of mostly woodland and lake front. The price was $140,000 and I wouldn't have to put any money down or deal with a bank. Clyde would give me the mortgage himself. The only catch was that I had to take possession with everything in it. At ninety-six, he didn't intend to move anything. I quickly agreed.

We moved in. It took a while. Clyde was a frugal old Vermonter and he saved everything. Closets had plastic bags full of hundreds of pairs of rolled up men's underwear. There were stacks and stacks of ledgers going back half a century. We had a bonfire in the yard and burned what we could; hauled everything else to the dump. There were old photos, a younger Clyde and another man. The two of them always. It was only through those and asking questions of people who had been in town a long time, that I pieced together his story.

Clyde had owned a hardware store in Barre, Vermont starting in 1936 and until the 1980s. His business partner was Norman Bryant. It was one of those crazy places that like his house was full of things and they were the only ones who knew where to find stuff. What most customers didn't know, however, was that Clyde and Norman also lived together. Also starting in 1936 and until Norman's death a few years before I met Clyde. In town they were known as the two bachelors who lived above the pond. Of course, they were much more than that. They were a great love story in a time that didn't allow them to be that, outside of the walls of that old house.

I think that's why that house had such good juju. There was a lot of love in it. Three years after I bought it, I decided to move back to Montpelier. I wanted to write about it, and I think I needed to leave to be able to do it. It's the setting for my first novel, *Mirror Lake*. These days, I have a camp nearby and I often walk by it, like I did the other day and when I do, I often imagine Clyde and Norman there, in a sanctuary from a world too bigoted to accept them, but in a town, at least, that left them alone.

As for Clyde, he died a year after I bought the house. The official record said it was natural causes, but I'm pretty sure it was a broken heart. He lived his last years as a pauper in that house. But his will contained assets of 20 million dollars. He left it all to the church.

On Baseball

The other day, I said to my daughter, I'm tired. These late-night Red Sox games.

Dripping with all the sardonic fever her teenage self could summon, she said, Baseball? Is that still a thing?

I once took her to a game, though, when she was six. Nine years ago. It was April and at Fenway. Because it was so early in the season, I was able to splurge for the best seats I had ever had. Three rows back, visiting team batting circle. In fact, they were almost too good, as this was before they put the netting up, and I spent the early innings on guard for a line drive that might end our lives.

Sox were playing the A's. Jon Lester was pitching. Bluebird spring day, if a little chilly. I wanted my girl to see how green that field was, what I remembered most when I first entered that park in 1978 or so, the romanticism of a game played without a clock in a cathedral. I wanted her to know the only religion I had ever believed in.

Instead, she liked that you could get ice cream brought to you where you sat, and she wanted a ball. Really wanted a ball.

Can we get a ball? She said. Maybe a foul one?

I kept explaining how that didn't happen, as we watched little boys over near the dugout storm the low fence near the dugout between innings doing this very thing, begging ball boys and ball girls to hand them one. I did some back of the envelope math. In any given game, there are thirty to forty foul balls? In a park that holds thirty-six thousand people. The odds are—well, I'm no good at math, so slightly north of zero.

Then in the 7th, Lester threw a fastball and an A's hitter fouled it far behind me. I stood up and turned around.

Suddenly I'm a hunter trying to feed my girl. I could see the ball. It looked like it was going to go out of the park behind us. It was that high. Really far away. But for some reason, inexplicably, I moved into the aisle, and began climbing the stairs and heading up toward the grandstands.

A moment of terror—I could see the ball now. It was still super high, but it was spinning backwards. I climbed maybe ten steps when I realized it was coming right at me. A spinning gyre. I was the twelve-year-old in little league not wanting the ball but it was finding me anyway. Fast. All around me, I heard the zombies rushing toward me. All thinking the same thing. Ball. I watched the seams. Spinning and spinning. I put my right hand out and holy shit it hurt but I caught it. I caught it clean. The zombies vanished. Collective groan.

Around me, the crowd roared. I brought the ball down to my girl. She beamed. Everyone said, nice job, dad.

But that's not the best part of this story.

An inning later, the seats in front of us, the second row, suddenly filled with the worst group of bros ever. Frat boys turned Wall Street, ties askew, day drunk with privilege and not caring about the expensive seats they didn't show up to sit in until the 8th inning to not only destroy our view but to spout vulgarities after vulgarities at a day game in front of my daughter.

Josh Donaldson was the A's third baseman. He was in the on-deck circle. Up close, Josh Donaldson was enormous. His biceps were bigger than my thighs. From some ten feet away, these bros are screaming at him. Hey Donaldson, fuck you. Hey Donaldson, sit the fuck down, we can't see the field. Hey Donaldson, you suck. Over and over. Donaldson, down in front.

Josh Donaldson suddenly turns around. He's all ripping muscle and his bat is in his hand menacingly. Up near his head. He walks toward these guys.

And I think he's going to come into the stands and destroy them. Like a Viking.

But instead, he says, sotto voce, Gentlemen, my manager requires us to stand in the on-deck circle and time our swings. In other words, I can't get down. I hope you understand. I'm trying to do my job.

Also, he says, his voice rising now above a whisper, but still gentle, I doubt you would like it if I showed up where you work and shouted F bombs at you when we didn't know each other. Have a little respect, okay? Do you understand? There are kids here.

They all shut up. My daughter held her shiny new ball. She may not think it's a thing, but she still has it. Somewhere in her messy room. My hand was swollen for days. I didn't care.

Magic

I was telling a friend of mine tonight over dinner outside about how there used to be this big beautiful great blue heron that flew by this part of the lake and my cabin every night around six. But it hadn't happened in a few years, maybe three. And how I missed that bird.

And then I segued into telling her the stories I used to tell my daughter when she was little, stories I intend to write someday, a quest story about a harmonica playing skunk and a curmudgeonly squirrel and a jolly raccoon and a one-eyed bear named Cyclops. But that the Great Blue heron had a small but important role in the stories, for every time he flew by, he shouted, in his stentorian Heron voice, Don't Believe the Turtle!

And this was important because as everyone knows, turtles are liars. In my narrative, it starts with denying they are even turtles, claiming instead that they are shell sharks, and therefore very scary and dangerous.

Equally important was why I told these stories to my daughter, Sarah. When she was three, we were expecting her little sister who we had already decided to name Jane. The pregnancy had been rocky and one day we were in the hospital having an ultrasound. My wife was twenty-three weeks. I saw the look on the technician's face—a cloud came over it, and she rushed out of the room. Moments later, a nurse was pushing my wife through the gleaming hallways to the maternity ward. The nurse was crying, which is never a good sign.

My wife's water had broken. The baby—or infection— we were told was coming and soon. The goal was to hang on as long as possible. A wide-faced NICU doctor spouted grim statistics at us, chances of survival, etc., and as I would learn later, in situations like this your mind moves like a scalpel to what you really need to know in the immediate.

My wife wasn't leaving the hospital until the baby came. There's nothing I can say in writing that would adequately express to you, even now, looking back over a windswept period knowing everything I know, including that the two of us are no longer together, how strong a woman she was and is. She hung on for almost a month on bed rest in the hospital until Jane was born, which might as well be an eternity under those circumstances. At birth, Jane weighed one pound, fourteen ounces. She looked like a cricket when I first saw her on the table surrounded by doctors and nurses. Later, Jane would become a beautiful, brown-eyed baby. She lived for six months, which honestly was a miracle. She fought like hell and almost made it.

As for that day, all of this meant in that moment was that I was going home to a three-year-old blonde girl with big blue eyes who wouldn't understand why her mother was now forty miles away and wouldn't be coming home for a while.

I must confess I hadn't been much of a parent to this point. We had a division of labor, Tia, and I—I was starting a college, and now running one, and trying, also, to write my fourth novel. I was insanely busy. I traveled a lot. Gave speeches. Raised money. To Sarah, our first daughter, I was the guy who showed up at dinner, made it (at least this, he cooks!) and then disappeared afterward with a kiss on the forehead back to an evening of phone calls.

And suddenly, it was just the two of us.

Sarah was inconsolable. She wanted her mother.

I remember a night in her bedroom. She's three. I desperately want her to go to bed, goddamn please, but she is a crazy person. Her long blonde hair, her eyes, wild, throwing clothes in the air, won't stop crying.

Look, I said, pointing.

What? She said, bleary from tears.

Mr. George Mouse, I said.

Who? She spat back, indignant.

Mr. George Mouse, I just saw him.

Where?

I gestured to a pile of clothes on the floor. You didn't hear him?

She wiped her eyes. Considered me. No.

I said, I was surprised I did. Usually, adults can't hear him or speak mouse. But I heard him say, hello, Sarah, him is right there.

Who is him?

Me, I said, don't you know? Animals only know the names of children. Adults they only call him or her. The reason is when you get too old you stop believing in magic.

My daughter looked up at me now, rolled onto the lower level of her bunk beds, and started sucking her thumb. She wasn't crying anymore, and she hadn't brushed her teeth, but screw it, cavities weren't my concern, not now.

Where does he live?

Mr. George Mouse?

Yes.

One Laundry Place, I said. Mr. George Mouse says, him doesn't even know where that is.

She didn't get the joke, but it hardly mattered. The stories grew from there and became more elaborate. Mr. George Mouse narrated the quest story I told her over and over, every single night. And I learned that stories could do a lot of things—well, I suppose I had always known that. I knew they could inspire. They could even start a new college. In the Irish tradition, they could keep people alive after they were gone. What I didn't know until that night was that they could make a father become a dad.

Sitting outside tonight, watching the fading sun reflect off the water, I then told my friend that years later when Sarah was like seven, she said to a friend of hers in front of me, my dad can talk to animals.

And her friend gave me shade, looked me up and down and then said soberly, yeah, I heard that.

We laughed heartily at that. The magic of small children when they still believe.

And as we laughed, to my right the Great Blue heron suddenly appeared for the first time in years as if this story had summoned it. It soared over the trees and swooped low in a glide past where we sat. Magnificent.

I said, holy shit, look, and it pumped its wings as it followed the slender expanse of lake away from us.

I shook my head. Big smile on my face.

It was a few minutes after six.

I wondered if the heron was Jane.

Neighborhood Boy #2

y favorite neighborhood kid, the seven-year-old fearless boy, came by yesterday when I was writing on my porch. I hadn't seen him in weeks. He was on a skateboard and wore a helmet and knee pads. I looked up from my laptop and he was suddenly there, doing tricks off the curb, and when I said, hey, buddy, he acted surprised that I was there, which he wasn't of course. He knew where to find me.

Where you been? I said.

Skateboard camp, he said proudly, doing a tiny spin in the air and landing back on the board.

Cool. That must have been fun.

It was awesome.

Hey, do you have a new little sister? I remember you said she was coming in August.

He smiled. We're having her today.

Oh wow. Amazing.

My mom will be home tonight with her. I'm glad she's a girl. Cause then she'll have a cool name.

That's kind of true, isn't it? Girl names are more musical or something. Like Diana. Or Sarah. Rather than, I don't know: Todd.

Yeah, he said, bored with this idea. Hey, Tom, he said, pointing at another house on the street. My friend lives there.

I see you guys hanging out sometimes.

He's a good friend. He doesn't smile. He's not a smiler.

Oh, I wonder why not?

Cause he has a triangle face.

Wait, what?

You know, his face is like a triangle but with hair on top.

I've never heard that.

Yeah, you have a round face. There are square faces, too. Triangle faces are just as nice as everyone else. They're just not smilers.

Thank you for telling me that, I said. And then I smiled.

The Ghost in You

Today I was walking in the wooded hilly park here with my friend, Dave, and Hugo, my hundred-pound Fox Red Labrador, when on a trail, we came across a woman in the woods. She wasn't on the trail, but twenty yards or so off it in a grove of trees, which is unusual since people pretty much walk on the defined trails up there. She was also, from our distance, quite elderly, easily eighty years old, and had on an ankle-length long-sleeved blue dress, not exactly hiking clothes. And this was not easy terrain.

Now Hugo, who will bark at people from within my house until they open the door, had never ever barked at another person before outside. If he sees people in the park, he often approaches them with his tail hugely wagging and a big dumb smile on his face. He wants to be patted. Given a treat. Told it's funny he has a ball or an apple in his mouth. But seeing her, Hugo suddenly grew still, his tail stiffened flat behind him, the hair rose on his back, he took a few steps off the path toward her and for the first time in the five years I've known him, he growled at a person.

Now we were still walking this whole time, and so was she, parallel to us, though unlike us, not on a trail and in heavy brush. I was trying to get Hugo to ignore her—I had said hello and she hadn't responded—when suddenly I realized she was singing. I couldn't make out her words, they were lilting and incantatory, and Hugo was now terrified. I've never seen him so scared. He barked at her. She kept moving toward us singing. Hugo turned and ran in front of us, whining, his ears low against his head, his body low to the ground.

Dave and I kept walking, not looking back. Behind us, we heard her faint sing-song voice.

"Is she a witch?" Dave said. "Something's not right there."

"I don't know," I said; I didn't. It occurred to me that she could be someone with dementia. That maybe someone would report an old woman missing later. With that in mind, I turned and snapped a photo of her where she stood in the grove of trees with my phone. She was oblivious to us so I didn't think she would mind. I forgot about the photo until later when I went to find a different one. When I looked at it, all I saw was the trees and the dappled autumn light coming through them. There was no woman to be seen.

Old Women Are the Funniest People

his morning I walked on the dirt roads near my lake house. It gets rural quick out here, and you go long stretches not seeing any houses. Just me and Hugo, the deer flies, the peepers in the wetlands next to the road. To the extent there are houses, you often can't see them, they are up and above and hidden. All you see is where the curve of the driveway meets the road. A mailbox. Nothing else.

On one of these, I came across an elderly woman standing at the end of her driveway. She was quite beautiful—striking really. She had a mane of full silver hair that fell halfway down her back. The pale blue eyes of a wolf. The summer day was warm, but she had on a long-sleeved gray dress and mud boots that went to her knees. In one hand, she held a broom.

Morning, I said. How are you?

She smiled and then laughed. Her eyes twinkled.

She said, oh, you know, just taking my broom out for a spin.

Life Goals

My closest neighbors at the lake are amazing people. Right next to me is a couple in their seventies. We've become close friends over the years. I marvel at them. They go on long mountain bike rides together. They swim all day, and she, regardless of the weather, swims the entire length of the lake every morning, which is no joke. They're retired and their kids are elsewhere, though come to visit often. But the thing I love the most about them is that after a full day of activity, at around five thirty every night, they get into their boat, a 1973 Boston Whaler, and they have a plate of cheese and crackers and glasses of white wine. And they steam slowly away from the dock, toward the bigger part of the lake, both standing, and he drives with her arm around him as they go.

Now, the cove we live in has many virtues. No fast boats

come in here. But the hills are steep behind us, and we get the morning sun, but not the afternoon, a contrast that becomes more visible at the end of the season. Our part of the lake, we know it's coming to an end before others do.

One time many years ago, I told them I loved their ritual, that they did this every day.

And he said to me, don't you see what we're doing? We're chasing the sun! We're making the day longer!

Nobody Recognizes Poets

In May of 1993, I was about to graduate from Hobart College in Geneva, New York with a degree in creative writing. The late and renowned Vermont poet and playwright David Budbill visited the college and gave a talk and a reading. I was one of hundreds in the audience.

While I was in school, I had a job at a winery. The winery was on the other side of massive Seneca Lake from the campus, about a twenty-minute drive, but it might as well have been a world away. It was a tiny place, a mom-and-pop, ten acres of grapes that went down to the lakeside, while all around it was surrounded by cornfields. The owners had a house at one end of the vineyards, and on the other was a small winery built into a hillside. There was no electricity. I was the only employee then. A long dirt road led through the cornfields from the main road to the winery, and on weekends we would get some traffic, tourists from Canada mostly, and my job was to pour them wine and talk about it, trying to sell the cases. The owners did all the other work. On non weekends, I would usually not see anyone, and I would spend my days putting labels on the bottles, corking them, and reading.

Anyway, the day after Budbill spoke I was working, the only one there. It was warm and sunny, and I was sitting out in front of the small winery built into the side of the hill with a book when I heard tires on the dirt road. I stood up and I saw a small Subaru snaking its way down through the cornfields. It reached me, and parked. A small, balding gray-haired man with a mustache got out. He looked around, and then looked at me, and I said, You're David Budbill.

His eyes grew wide. Poets aren't used to being recognized. Especially in the middle of nowhere. And far from home.

How do you know who I am?

I was at the reading last night.

He looked relieved. Oh. You're a student. Why were so many people there? The place was packed.

It was required for English majors.

I wish you hadn't told me that, he said.

He was staying another night in the area, and he liked wine. He was my only customer that day. I gave him the full tasting—the cabernets and the merlots and pinots and the chardonnays, etc. I joined him for a couple. He was very gruff, but we talked. He asked if I was a writer; this felt generous since I was twenty-three and hadn't done anything. I said I wrote short stories, but none published. I was a good salesman and I got him to buy a mixed case and he went on his way.

At that point, my post-graduation plan was up in the air. I was broke. In short succession, though, my girlfriend at the time got into a grad program at Goddard College in Vermont, and I won a writing award at graduation that came with a five-thousand-dollar prize. We moved to Vermont in June. I brought my limited resumé to every storefront in town. I ended up, rather quickly, getting hired at what was then Vermont College, part of Norwich University, in the admissions office.

A week after I began work, I was asked to join a search committee for new faculty in the undergrad program that was there then. One of the first people we interviewed was David Budbill. When he sat down at the table, he looked around at the six or so people, and then his eyes settled on me. He looked very puzzled. It threw him off.

I said preemptively, We met a month ago. At a vineyard in upstate New York.

He just nodded. But then after the interview, I ran into

him in the hallway. He stopped me. He said, You're starting to freak me out, kid. Who the fuck are you?

Years later, shortly before his death, I had the honor of hosting David and his wife at an event at the college. I was the president now, and the college was now independent. Twenty-two years had passed. His wife is a painter and I own one of her pieces. I talked first about how much I loved her art and then I told them this story. They both listened intently. His wife laughed heartily.

David Budbill said, I don't remember you at all.

Strangers

I love days when it's warm enough that I can work on my porch instead of my kitchen. I live in a neighborhood close to downtown Montpelier, Vermont, a neighborhood of old Victorians, a front porch culture, and one that has a surprising amount of foot traffic, especially during Covid-19. Women pushing strollers; children riding bikes; people walking their dogs, etc. Sometimes people see me working and say hello, other times they don't.

Yesterday I watched as a middle-aged man with a thick head of gray hair came running down the middle of the street, jogging at a pretty good clip. Coming the other way, also in the middle of the road, was a brown-haired middle-aged woman, also running at a good clip. As they went to pass each other, they both suddenly stopped. Wordlessly they stood there for a moment, and then I believe it was her who moved in and took his face in her hands, while he put his hand on the back of her head, and suddenly they kissed, passionately and intensely. Then they pulled apart from each other and started to run in their respective directions.

I couldn't let this go. I tripped into their moment.

I shouted, I thought you were strangers! They both looked up to where I sat on the porch, at a table in front of my laptop, seeing me for the first time.

Without breaking stride, moving away from each other, they shouted back in unison, We are!

The Only List I Will Ever Make

1. I don't care who you love, just love.
2. While we're on love, don't hate. Hate is corrosive. I mean, some people, okay, you might have to hate. But don't waste time on petty hate—like artists you don't like or admire. Just ignore them. Let them be.
3. Find your people and protect them like it's your job.
4. Tip. Tip like your child is on the other side of the counter and they need that last bit to knock out the rent. The benefit will come back to you in spades.
5. If you can dream it, you can become it.
6. Listen to children. They still hear magic.
7. All practices pale in comparison to cooking when you get right down to it. Feed as many people who will let you. Food is love.
8. Tell stories. In the end, it's all we are. Better yet, channel them. They're all around us if we just pay attention.

9. Dogs will make you better. Cats will make you glad they're tiny.
10. Fail. Stumble. Trip. It's the only way you fly.
11. Call your mom. If your mom is no longer here, call her anyway. No one will root for you more.

Neighborhood Boy #3

took a long walk today around my almost empty little city. I had spent the morning writing, as best as I could, though the effort felt half-hearted as writing fiction does when around you the American experiment feels like it's failing, this time, for real. I wanted to walk because walking is an antidote to sadness. If we are doing the simple things, one foot in front of the other, head up, watching where we are going, the sadness doesn't go away, but it becomes a low note for a moment, there but in the background, the pluck of a bass.

Back home, I sat on my porch, and I thought about how small my world had become. I haven't put gas in my car since February. It's now June. I walk these streets and up to the park. I'm privileged, I know, I can stay home and write. I'm safe. My family is safe. And I was sitting there when the seven-year-old I admire because he's right out of 1978, totally free range, pulls up on his bike in front of my porch and says, Hey, Tom, how old are you?

Fifty-one.

Wow, you're like super-duper old.

I know.

I heard there's one lady who lived to a hundred.

There are many who do, buddy.

Hey, do you have a bike?

I don't, I said.

He thought about this. Well, maybe, he said, you'll get one for your birthday. Or for Christmas.

I laughed hard. That would be awesome, I said.

If you do, we could race, though I would let you win the first one.

You know what? I said. I wouldn't race you. You're way too good. Like seriously.

Thanks, man, he said, and he turned and rode away, and he pedaled hard toward the other side of the street and tried to jump the curb, but he hit it wrong, his front tire not square, and it went badly. I watched him fly over the handlebars and skid across the pavement on his elbows.

I stood up and I saw him rise on his feet. He looked like he was about to cry but was holding it in. His voice, when he spoke, was very quiet. Don't come over here, he said. I'm okay.

You sure, buddy?

He lifted one elbow and looked at it. His voice was stronger now. This one is good, he said. He lifted the other one, and said, uh oh. This one needs work. I'll be back, Tom, okay?

Of course, buddy.

Ten minutes later he came ripping by on a scooter. He looked up at me as he went past. The wind blew back his hair. I mean, he was flying. Fearless.

I got some Band-Aids, he yelled.

Go Your Own Way

n my now yearlong pandemic sibling text thread today, we started talking about cars, and iconic cars from our childhood. We were trying to remember the wagon we had in the 70s and my brother, Richard, who has the best memory of all of us, pulled that it was a 1972 Dodge Monaco station wagon. It fit all nine of us. My mom and dad and their seven children. Three in front, four in back, me and Dan, the littles, in the way back.

My greatest memory of this car doesn't include my parents though. It was summer. I think 1977. Worcester, Massachusetts. Our parents wanted us out of the house. They gave my oldest brother, the only one with a license, the keys and twenty bucks and said take everyone to McDonalds. We climbed in. The day was warm and breezy. All the windows were down. We sat in order of age. Steve driving, Kathy riding shotgun; Maura, Richard, and David, left to right on the back bench seat; me and Dan in the way back.

Even our window, the very back one, was down, and we were laying down with our backs against the back seat, looking at the cars behind us. You only wore seatbelts in the front seat then, if at all. This might have been the first time all of us were out in the world without our parents. The breeze was blowing warm through the windows, and we all had long hair like rock stars and the wind blew it back and across our faces.

On the radio came that summer's biggest hit. Fleetwood Mac's "Go Your Own Way." I don't know who started singing first, it certainly wasn't me, but it moved through the cab of that long, tinny wagon. My brother drove fast. We hit the chorus. Seven voices rose as one. They were, mostly, older than me. We ranged from seventeen to nine. Sometimes we fought. Some of us got along better than others. But for a moment, in that boat speeding through the streets in the meat of summer, we were all doing the same thing.

Pandemic Shopping

All my smoke alarms died at once the other day, relentless chirping that drove Hugo, my dog, crazy. Yesterday I went to the hardware store and the stoner kid with his hair concealing his eyes showed me where the smoke alarms were. He stood watch a few feet away as I went to grab three of them and he said to me, Dude.

What?

He looked back toward the desk where his co-workers were. And then back to me. In a half whisper he said, Not those, dude. You don't want those.

Why?

His voice was quiet. He said, Because they talk, man.

I looked at the box. It said TALKING ALARM on the top.

Oh, but by talk it just means it says THERE'S SMOKE

IN THE HALLWAY, when there's smoke in the hallway.

You don't know that, man. What if it talks at other times? What if it says other stuff? Some things just shouldn't talk.

I nodded. I see your point, I said, and I bought three that didn't talk, and just had a standard alarm.

Only when I got home, I realized they couldn't be hardwired, so I must bring them back today.

I'm going to tell him they started to talk in the middle of the night.

Raising Wolves

eisha was the first dog that I called my own. I deliberately don't say I owned her, because even though I took her in when she was a puppy, she was unownable. Half timber wolf, and the rest a mix of Samoyed and Husky, she was bred to be a sled dog but was too big. They could tell that when she was seven weeks old. The wolf was strong in her, as was the Alpha female.

Back then, my girlfriend and I lived in this 1790s red house in the middle of the woods. Keisha would disappear for hours at a time and when she came back, she often had another dog's bowl in her mouth, which in the dog world is the ultimate you are my bitch statement. I got your food bowl. What are you going to do?

She never wanted to be inside, especially in winter. She had webbed feet for running through snow. I remember how she liked to sit on this little knoll that gave her a view of the dirt road. She would lay there like a Sphinx and in snowstorms the snow would just cover her until you could barely make her out.

Maybe it's because I was young and stupid, or maybe it was because both my girlfriend and I were in grad school and lost and I was dreaming of being a writer, but we didn't get her spayed.

The first time she was in heat was winter. One night, the coyotes came for her. Their cries were like children when they were distant but soon, they were circling the house, a pack of them, and their cries went right through us. It was one of those ten below nights with only a moon in the clear sky. The coyotes were running around the house and inside Keisha was losing her mind, literally throwing herself at the door, wanting to run with them. It was the only time she ever growled at me. I just shook my head at her and said, No. The next day, in the sunshine, you could see the path the coyotes beat around the house, snow trampled flat, here and there, flecks of blood.

The second time she was in heat was the summer. One day a pickup truck pulled in my driveway. A guy I didn't know got out and he asked me if I had seen his dog. I had not. He introduced himself—told me his name was Merlin and his dog was Vinnie. I didn't say it, but it seemed to me it should have been the other way around. He asked me if

I had a dog. I did, I said. He asked me if she was in heat. How did you know? Cause Vinnie headed this way. Vinnie knocks up all the females. He's here, he said.

I haven't seen him. Merlin whistled then, and the bushes behind me, the ones right next to my front door, moved, and out stepped this enormous yellow lab. Get over here, Merlin said. Vinnie jumped in the back of the truck they left.

But two mornings later, Vinnie was successful. He laid in wait in the woods, and it happened fast.

She was pregnant. A little later that summer, my girlfriend and I drove to Prince Edward Island where we had rented a cottage for a week. It was an eighteen-hour drive. We thought Keisha was maybe a month away from giving birth and we left her behind with a dear friend who agreed to house sit. A few days into our vacation, the potato farmer across the street knocked on the door.

I got good news and I got bad news, he said. The good news is your dog had nine puppies. The bad news is she disappeared with them.

What do you mean disappeared?

That's all I know. You got to go home.

Keisha gave birth in the mudroom the night after we left. My friend set her up on a blanket and all went well until he went to sleep. Then she broke the window with her head and one by one, by the scruff of their necks, brought those puppies deep into the woods where she built a den at the base of a tree. While we were driving home, he found her. She had been out there for days. A vet came. Two of the puppies had died, seven were alive, and she was badly infected. Back home, the vet told me, she will be okay, but she can't nurse. We should put the puppies down. Otherwise, the option is that you hand nurse them twenty-fours a day. Once a dog stops nursing, she said, they won't go back. They reject them. You'll have to do this for weeks and weeks.

I said, we'll do it. And we did. We hand nursed them. Little bottles like babies get. They were white and black dogs. Hamsters. And then something amazing happened. Keisha healed. She climbed in with them, and she let them nurse. She started over. And weeks later I would come home from work when the seven of them were bigger, and they were out in the yard in a makeshift pen, and they'd all move to the fence of it like sparrows when they saw me, and I'd open it and pretend to run away while they streamed after me, giving up and collapsing on the lawn and letting those puppies wash their big wet tongues all over my face.

Silent Night

On Christmas Eve 1968, my father was thirty-seven years old, and my mother was thirty-six. They had six children. I was the youngest, three months old that night. My younger brother, Dan, their seventh, was yet an idea. He would be born a year later, the day after Christmas, 1969.

They were insanely busy people. My mother dealt with these six kids full time, while my dad, like my mother, a first-generation college graduate, taught history full time at Worcester Polytech Institute while getting his doctorate at Boston University and doing various odd jobs to make it all work and pay the bills for this burgeoning family.

That night, after all their children were in bed, they divided the labor that neither of them was particularly good at. While in the basement my mother assembled a doll house, my father went to the attic where he labored to put together three bicycles to put under the tree. Up in the attic, he brought a radio with him, and on it, the news was narrating the Apollo 8 mission, when astronauts, Jim Borman, Jim Lovell, and Bill Anders became the first humans to orbit the moon.

At one point, and by now it's late and my father is exhausted, the news announcer says that the three men are going to be on the dark side of the moon and will be out of radio reach for five minutes. He cites a bible passage and says they will go silent until they hear from them again.

My father stops working. He sits down. From the transistor radio comes the soft blare of static. Silence can be both deafening and eternal. In front of him are the unfinished bikes, so terrestrial, while above, in the milky dark, men are on the other side of another world.

Five minutes seems like an hour. Then a voice, Houston, we're back.

My father sighs and goes back to work. By the time he and my mom finish, it's 5 A.M. My mom has a brainstorm. They've been awake for almost twenty-four hours. Let's wake the kids now, she says. They can open their presents and then while they play with their toys, we can go back to sleep. The older ones can watch Tommy (me.)

They wake the six children for an early Christmas. Were the children excited for this early gift?

Santa was already here?

Wait till you see!

No, they were pissed. Cranky and furious.

I heard this story for the first time tonight on our family Zoom, on a night when we would usually be all together eating and celebrating. I share it for all those hardworking moms and dads kicking some butt tonight, staying up late, putting stuff together, going the extra mile for kids who might not fully understand what you do for them, the sacrifices you make, but trust me, they will in time. As I have.

Proud

Not long before Covid-19 hit, back when we could be shoulder to shoulder with people, when I used to go out just to find a conversation and some stories after a day of writing, I was having a beer with a friend at Three Penny Taproom. It was packed. Two deep at the bar. The back wall lined with legislators. A Friday night. My friend is a Jamaican immigrant. He paints houses for a living. We were in the middle of a conversation about sports when his phone started to vibrate and buzz on the wood of the bar.

Oh, that's my daughter, he said, and he answered right there in the noisy bar.

What? He shouted. You got into Harvard?

And then he turned to the entire noisy bar, taking the phone off his ear, his voice, mostly, lost in the din of music and glasses being shuffled across the wood and loud conversation.

My daughter got into Harvard! He yelled.

That's fantastic, I said.

He yelled it again and now his energy was so kinetic, he couldn't contain himself. He was off his stool and running down the length of the bar holding his phone in the air and yelling, My daughter got into Harvard!!!

He ran back and forth yelling it. Holding his phone out.

I watched as slowly others became aware of the profound pride of this dad, who was going to make sure everyone knew about it. It was one of the purist expressions of joy I have ever seen.

And because we're a small town, and we all know each other, the bartender heard what he was saying and began to clang a large bell that was behind the bar in celebration, presumably for moments like this. And because of that, even over the music, everyone heard him.

My daughter got into Harvard!

And for a moment all the individual conversations stopped, and everyone paid attention to this simple fact. And at once, suddenly, everyone clapped, louder and louder, and my friend held out his phone so his daughter could hear it.

She worked her ass off, he yelled. Four years of a straight As.

And, you know, when it comes to this pandemic, the loss of life is what matters the most. That can't be forgiven, ever. But smaller things are lost, too. Clean, well-lighted places. A shared celebration. A Black girl from Vermont, the daughter of an immigrant without any money, going to Harvard because she earned it.

Neighborhood Boy #4

Writing on my porch in Montpelier, summer rain falling hard in the neighborhood. My seven-year-old bike-riding friend comes running by barefoot with his older sister, who is maybe nine. Preemptively, they say to me, as if I might have some authority, we're allowed to play in the rain.

Awesome, I say.

They go across to another house and yell and a boy emerges from the back door, also barefoot. They yell at him: we're playing in the rain.

Me too, he says, running out like he has been all along, and he grabs a scooter and starts to circle both.

The new boy says to the girl, hey, you got a haircut.

She says, why would you say anything when I only cut two inches?

He says, you look like Dora the Explorer.

She says, I don't know who that is.

He says, how can you not know?

Her little brother, rising to her defense, says, hey man she doesn't know.

New boy says, who is stronger, you or your sister?

Rain is dumping now. Little brother rises and goes to his sister and tries to push her off her mark, like Sumo, but she holds firm and pushes back and he falls hard on the pavement.

Are you okay? She says.

He stands up, brushes off his arms, shrugs. Yeah, he says.

New boy says, I guess she's stronger.

I guess, little brother says. This time. But I don't know karate yet.

Hey, the girl says, did you mean it?

Mean what?

That I look like her. Dora whoever.

Yeah, new boy says. You do.

She turns away so he won't see her smile.

Circles

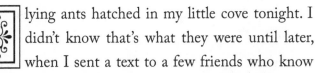lying ants hatched in my little cove tonight. I didn't know that's what they were until later, when I sent a text to a few friends who know these things asking them what was hatching. I was writing. Working on revisions. The grind. I stood and the sun had emerged, and I decided to go for a swim to stretch. It was only then that I noticed the surface of the water was covered with thousands and thousands of bugs. There are often bugs on top of the water, but this was different. It didn't really matter as they kind of parted for me as I swam. When I got out, back to the deck, drying off, bass and trout, who I never really see as more than ripples on the lake, were rising to eat the flying ants, sometimes coming out of the water like small dolphins. A kingfisher perched on a pine branch to my right swooped and dove and caught pumpkinseeds in its mouth and flew to a tree on

the opposite shore to swallow them. Outside my screened-in porch a spider's elaborate web is suddenly full of the flying ants, the spider, fat and wooly, patiently watching as if surprised by this gift. The loons swim into the cove. Not just a pair but eleven of them. A gathering, like I had never seen. Circling each other, a meeting called by someone. Sometimes rising with a great flapping of wings to make a point. My neighbor shouts to me that it's a bad sign and could mean a long winter. That it's only mid-August and they're already talking about hitting the road for what else could they be talking about?

I have no idea. I don't speak loon. The sun sets. Now the bats are out. They dive like fluttering paper airplanes in front of the deck, thankfully eating mosquitoes. Venus is above the hills. Everyone else is gone except for me and Hugo. And neither of us fly. Not really.

Being John Turtorro

A year or so after we launched our graduate film school at VCFA, the iconic actor John Turturro got in touch through a Brooklyn screenwriter friend involved in the program and said he would love to come up and show one of his films and meet with students.

I had been a fan of his forever. *Do the Right Thing*, *Barton Fink*, *Quiz Show* and of course, his role as the nemesis, Jesus, to *The Big Lebowski*.

And on and on. So, we quickly said yes. John flew to Burlington on an October afternoon. He would show his film at seven at the Savoy Theater and take questions afterward. But before, I decided I would throw a party for him at my house. I invited faculty and staff and local VIPs. Trustees were there. The mayor. City officials. All of us, admittedly, a little small-town star-struck by having this Hollywood actor in our midst. I had it catered, a giant spread of food across a huge table. A full bar. John was scheduled to arrive around four thirty, and by four my house was full of people, eating and drinking and waiting for the car with Mr. Turtorro to arrive.

Well, when John arrived, he came through the kitchen, saw the crowd before anyone saw him, and ducked into what was my daughter's, who was maybe six at the time, playroom. One of my staff told me he had done that, and I opened the door to find him in one of those tiny chairs little kids use in kindergarten, wooden and painted, and facing the wall with his back to me. I went over and he said, who are you? It sounded more like, who you?

He said this without ever making eye contact with me.

And I told him, I'm Tom Greene, we talked on the phone, I'm the president of VCFA, and this is my house.

He said, Oh, Tom, okay. Thank you. Do you mind if I just stay here for a bit? I have some things I need to do on my phone.

Of course, whatever you need.

I left him alone. But the thing was, he never came out. The party went on without him and people were aware he was in this other room, and wanted to meet him but after a while, it became clear, through several conversations I had with him, that he would not be coming out. And this became a thing: Is he coming out? No, I don't think so. So he won't be coming out? I think he's busy on his phone. Hours went by. And he stayed put. He had to be the shyest, most introverted person I had ever met.

By then, it was time for his film to be shown and the party emptied out because everyone was going to the showing. Only then did John emerge from my child's playroom and that tiny chair, and we took him downtown where his film was shown and where, after, he stood up and spoke and took questions. He was a different man. He was alive on stage—funny, charismatic, a presence who made the room small and every questioner heard and valued.

Afterwards, a small group of us and John left the theater. Everyone was telling him how amazing that was. But he looked at me and said, Tom, I need to eat.

I said, Okay, it's late for Montpelier—it was like nine thirty—but I'm sure we can find something.

Of course, we had had that party where he never emerged, and that giant spread of food.

But John said to me, I need a pizza, Tom, a whole pizza.

It was a cool October night, and I was thinking in my head what was open.

I need a pizza, a whole pizza, John said again. Is there an Italian place?

There's Positive Pie? But not sure they're still serving.

I need a pizza, a whole pizza, he said again. He said it maybe three more times.

Well, let's try.

So six of us went to Positive Pie. The issues were twofold: the kitchen was about to close, and it was the night before Halloween, and they were having a Halloween party. The place was packed with people drinking in costume.

I went up to the host stand and I didn't waste time. I said, can I talk to the manager?

A minute later this woman came over and she said, Can I help you?

I introduced myself and she said, Yes, I know who you are. I said, do you recognize the gentleman behind me?

She looked at him. Is he an actor?

Yes, that's John Turtorro. And he really wants to eat at your restaurant. And if I can't get him a pizza, and a whole pizza, everything's going to fall apart.

Let me see what I can do, she said.

And like a total badass she went over to a table of bros drinking IPAs in ironic costumes and told them if they gave up their table and drank from the bar, their drinks for the rest of the night were on her.

We had a table. John not only got his pizza, a whole pizza, but several of them and along with a few bottles of red wine, he finally seemed like he was enjoying himself.

We were all telling stories. I remember telling one, and I don't remember what it was, but John in his thick Brooklyn accent said, That's a good story. You're funny. That's a good story.

He never looked up when he said it. John's eyes were on the table, his pizza, his wine.

Meanwhile, around us, the Halloween party filled in. And then, coming in the door, I saw him. It was a guy dressed, immaculately, as the Big Lebowski. He had flowing hair, a huge robe, a beard, and at the bar he stopped for a White Russian. He had a blunt dangling from his mouth, and you could tell, even from a distance you could tell, that he had been waiting for Halloween for a long time. This was less a costume than it was method acting. A becoming.

The Dude was feeling it. He worked through the tables and even through the buzz and the noise, I thought I could almost hear the unique twang in Jeff Bridge's voice emanating from him.

And then he went past our table. Casually, strolling, scanning the room. I saw him turn, take me in, and then, to my left, Turtorro.

I saw the sea change in his face. The brittle mask of costume disappearing and under it the realization that maybe this wasn't a dream but was meant to be all along.

Jesus, he mouthed. Jesus, he mouthed again.

Holy shit. Jesus.

I walked John back to the Inn at Montpelier that night. By the time we left Positive Pie, word had spread he was in the room, and I wasn't envious of his celebrity, and I understood why he didn't make eye contact. Getting out of there was a gauntlet. People rushed him like zombies and over and over he just said the same thing, Thank you, thank you, very kind, thank you.

I left a huge tip. The next day I sent the manager a dozen roses. But the real winner of the night was the guy dressed as the Dude. For a moment, he became him.

Older Women Are the Funniest People #2

I was walking home the other day and a small group of couples, neighbors in their late sixties, were standing in the road having a socially distanced conversation. This was at the height of quarantine. One of my neighbors is a British lady, and she has a super-fast wit that I admire. Seeing me, she said, there he is. We're having a party.

You are? I said.

Yes, she said. We're celebrating the four-month anniversary of that blue children's glove sitting on your front steps.

Neighborhood Boy #5

eventy degrees today and I'm working outside. My favorite neighborhood kid whizzed up on his bike. I haven't talked to him since last October.

Hey, buddy, I said, how was your winter?

He shrugged. He had business on his mind.

Tom, he said, did you have a birthday since I saw you?

No, my birthday is in September. Why?

I was wondering if someone gave you a bike.

I laughed; I had forgotten this conversation from last year. I wished I lived in a world where someone gave me a bike, I thought.

No, buddy, no bike. I did get one for Christmas once.

Where is it?

Oh, that was a long time ago. When I was your age.

Did someone take it?

No, no. I probably outgrew it. It had a banana seat though.

His eyes widened. What? The seat was a banana?

I realized I had just gone from a hundred years old to a thousand years old, to a time when bikes were made from fruit.

No, I laughed. They called it that because the seat kind of looked like a banana. It was long and yellow and two people could sit on it.

I saw him digesting this. It must have been hard to do tricks, he said.

Yeah, it probably was.

Well, I hope someone gives you a bike. Then we could race.

I don't know. You'd win every time.

He agreed with this. I'd let you win sometimes, he said. That's how it works.

Quarantine

'**ve** been thinking that this living in the time of the virus felt familiar, and I couldn't put my finger on it until this morning. It's like grief. Even in moments of normalcy, small moments of grace, like today, when the sun hits your face and it's warm and you see a pair of cardinals in your yard, it's still there, sometimes in the background, sometimes more present, right in front of you. You can't escape it. Makes it hard to sleep, the usual stuff of living can take more effort, the simple pleasures aren't as simple anymore. But the good news is that the cure is time. We just got to keep doing the work. Making house, telling stories, keeping in touch, loving those you're meant to love, and loving yourself. And one day soon that fog will lift, when you least expect it, the sun will be really shining this time, everything green as a rainforest, and we'll remember what it's like to hug.

The Cagey Veteran

I n the fall of 2005, my third novel, *Envious Moon*, was about to come out. My publisher at the time, William Morrow, sent me to a big bookseller's conference in an Atlantic City casino to sign books. I had never been in a casino before. I arrived the night before and spent the evening just walking around, people watching. The giant windowless carpeted spaces, the smell of stale cigarettes, sad-faced Americans sitting on heavy haunches and wearing their despair-like clothes.

I didn't play any games—I never got the gambling bug, plus I didn't know the lingua Franca to engage and was afraid to embarrass myself. So, I had dinner at a steakhouse and retired to my room. In the morning I arrived at this cavernous ballroom full of tables representing different publishers. We had to be there at nine thirty, and doors were to open at ten. I shared a table with another writer from Morrow, a gentleman maybe ten or fifteen years older than me. He was self-effacing and seemed nervous to me. We had a half hour, so we talked. He had just written his first book. Since I was now a cagey veteran with three books under my belt, I decided I would use this time together to impart some of the things I had learned, some of the things other more experienced writers had taught me. I remember telling him that a book launch starts with winning the publishing house itself over.

Everyone must love it, I said, not just your editor but other editors, assistants, publicists. They need to know you, I said. Be especially nice to those who don't appear to have any power. They will fight for you. They're the ones who get things done.

He actually wrote that down.

You have a website? I asked.

Working on it.

You need that. It's not like we get a lot of fan mail, but you want a way for readers to reach you.

Got it, he said.

Around us, things started to get busier. Over the intercom, someone announced that the doors would be opening shortly.

What's your novel about, by the way? I asked him.

Oh, it's a memoir, he said. About my dog.

Oh, cool, I said, but in my mind, I thought, good luck with that.

The doors opened. A line formed at our table, and it snaked through the whole room, out into the hallway and into the main lobby of the casino. He must have signed seven hundred books. I signed around sixteen and half of those were people who I'm pretty sure felt bad for me.

His name was John Grogan. His book was *Marley & Me*.

Foraging

oday, deep in the park, I came across a guy hiking the other way. He greeted me like an old friend, though we didn't know each other. Check these out, he said, and out of all his pockets, he started pulling out mushrooms. Hen of the wood, chicken of the wood, lobsters, he said excitedly. Man. I'm going to my daughter's for dinner tonight and I said I'd bring an appetizer. Now I know what I'm doing.

I'm jealous, I told him.

Running into him jogged a memory. Almost twenty years ago, I was writing my second novel, *I'll Never Be Long Gone*. It's set in a restaurant. My friend, David Aronson, is one of those Vermonters who is good at everything— cooking, fly fishing, baking, hunting, stonework, sugaring, you name it. For a scene in the book, I asked him if I could tag along one day while he foraged for mushrooms. In my book, the protagonist, a chef, was going to take the woman he loved to find mushrooms, filling her, he hoped, with awe around the idea that there was food all around us, if you knew where to find it. That he knew how to find beauty.

We hiked deep into the forest that day, something that I didn't do often then. It was October, and the slanted light that came through the trees dappled the forest floor. As we walked, David read the land. On a south-facing hillside, he found what we were looking for.

There, in a forest of spruce and poplar and hemlock, was a field of chanterelles. At first, I didn't see them, but then they were everywhere. David showed me how to pick them sustainably, and as we filled a basket, he explained how they grew in veins, and I thought about this, like how apple trees in an orchard are all connected under the ground, roots touching each other like clasped hands.

That night, like my protagonist in the book would do, I cooked for the woman I loved then. I made a stock out of some of the chanterelle stems and some dried porcini. I sauteed the chanterelles in butter and garlic, and a sprig of rosemary for the woodsy flavor. I cooked arborio rice slowly in the stock, adding it a bit at a time, until the rice was al dente. At the end, I brought the rice and the chanterelles together, with a little more butter and some Parmigiano-Reggiano, some parsley for color.

Outside, the calendar was about to flip from fall to winter. The cool air redolent of woodsmoke. Inside, though, all you could smell was that bubbling risotto. I smelled it again today, coming to me across the years.

On Baseball #2

omorrow the Red Sox and Yankees meet for the first time in a one-game playoff since 1978. People, mostly in Massachusetts, remember that game as the time Bucky "fucking" Dent hit a home run to win it. It was an old school Fenway home run, a fly ball that would have been an out anywhere else but found its way into the net above the green monster.

I was ten. My younger brother, Dan, was nine. We skipped school to watch the game. We were raised on the three Rs: reading, religion, and Red Sox. Since the last two were blurred, we were mostly all Catholics and Red Sox fans. And none more than my grandmother. We watched it at her apartment.

She was born in 1899. In truth, she hadn't suffered as much as most of us. In her nineteenth year, 1918, she witnessed a World Series win. Though none since.

My grandma, Nora, liked to watch three things in her apartment: Laurence Welk, the front door security camera, and the Sox. She had a Yaz poster in her bathroom, and she loved Bill Lee, the spaceman, and I often wonder what she would have thought if she knew some forty years later Bill and I would both pose sort of naked to raise money for Vermont libraries. I like to think she would have laughed.

Anyway, what I remember about that game is of course, Bucky Dent's home run, but more readily, is her hero, Yastrzemski's, final out. For twenty five years or so, he had been their greatest hitter. His hair had gone gray. Men aged quicker in those days. Yaz loved beer and cigarettes. But he was a God and as Updike famously told us about Ted Williams refusing to tip his cap, Gods don't answer letters.

Down to their last out, the great Yastrzemski came to the plate for the Red Sox. They trailed by a run.

Not to worry, my grandma told us. He will fix this.

We all knew this to be true.

But then Yaz swung. Men were on first and third. He looked tired. Like someone's dad after a long week. The ball floated weakly toward third base. Lazy. Game over.

After, and fragile, broken, frankly, I looked at my grandmother, and she was stoic, though a single tear fell down the gutter of her cheek. Her hero, our hero, couldn't carry the day. Nothing could.

Nora died not long after that. Science will say her heart gave, though I still wonder if it gave a little that day and because of that day. She loved fiercely.

I don't know. Sports are vastly overrated as a shared experience. But sometimes they strike at the heart of what it means to be human.

Change

The seasons flip suddenly here. Labor Day. A single red leaf waves like a glove. For a time, the rain falls so hard that it goes sideways. The front that comes in after brings heavy, low leaden clouds that sit in a thick ribbon over the hills, blue sky above them like a fake promise. The grass in the yard is dewy. The air suddenly has the hint of winter in its breath.

Apples

n our walk this morning, Hugo, my giant red Labrador, found two wild apples that had fallen off trees on the sides of the dirt roads near the lake house. He ate one there and took the other home for later. I've never known a dog who loves apples so much. At my home in Montpelier, there is an apple tree that every other year produces small pale red apples. Hugo eats three or four a day in the fall, and the deer come down from the park to eat the rest.

One time my daughter and her mom were traveling abroad and their dog, Frida, was staying with me and Hugo. Frida is a great dog, intelligent as can be and sweet but she suffers serious separation anxiety when those two are away. This was in the fall. The first hour she was at my house, Frida kept whining and running to the door, climbing up it and looking out the window panicked and forlorn.

Seeing this, Hugo ran out the open back door into the yard. He returned a moment later with an apple in his mouth. He went over to Frida and laid it at her feet and stepped back.

She looked at him like, what is that? You eat those?

And he looked at her like, they always make me feel better.

She didn't eat the apple, but she settled down. Sometimes, to borrow from Ray Carver, all we need is a small, good thing.

Kindness

I stopped at the local Shaw's to get cat food. In front of me in line was a man in his seventies. I recognized him from around town. He has a roof over his head, but he often hangs out on the streets. Sits on benches. Pushes a cart. He put on the belt a tomato, some ground beef, a box of milk bones, a box of cereal, a jar of pickles. He had fourteen dollars. The price was more than that. He asked her to remove the tomato. Then the pickles. I was weighing doing something while also hearing the pride in his voice. I was going to say, let me take care of that, but something held me back, especially when he apologized to me for the delay.

You're fine, I said.

Right then, the man bagging the groceries, gray-haired, sturdy, around sixty, took his wallet out of his back pocket and opened it. I saw he had three single dollar bills in there. He fingered the three of them, removed them and wordlessly handed them to the older man who took them without saying anything, added them to his ten and four ones and slid them to the girl.

When I got up there, I said to the man bagging, that was really nice what you did. Wanted you to know I noticed.

He didn't make eye contact with me, and he didn't smile. When he spoke, I realized words weren't his thing. They came out haltingly. But what he said was, We all got to be friends.

A few weeks later I would see his photo in the local paper. He wasn't as old as I thought, in fact only a year older than me. They didn't say how he died. But they said he would be remembered by everyone for his remarkable kindness.

Tennis

everal years ago, I went on a date that was set up by a friend with someone I never met. This was in New York City. It was summer. I was staying at the Standard Hotel in the Meatpacking District. After a day of meetings, I had arranged to meet her for a drink at the Standard Grill outside. All I knew about her was that she ran her own small fashion company. When she showed up, she was tall and lovely and had a great smile.

Anyway, after we got past the initial awkwardness— the establishment that we were indeed the right people, the ordering of wine, etc.—we began the second phase of awkwardness, the conversation. I remember asking her what she liked to do when she wasn't working.

I play a lot of tennis, she said.

Oh, I play tennis. We should play sometime.

She laughed. No, no, we shouldn't.

Why not?

She folded her arms. It would be a bloodbath, she said. I would destroy you. I mean really destroy you. It would not be pretty. It would take you a long time to recover.

I don't know, I said. I'm pretty good. In fact, two years in a row I won the Central Vermont open division doubles tournament. Up at a place called First in Fitness. They have four indoor courts.

She smirked. Looked away for a moment and then fixed her eyes on me. I beat Kim Clijsters when she was number one in the world. I once took Serena Williams to three sets.

I paused, took this in.

That sounds impressive, I said, and then I shrugged. Maybe I'm missing something, but it sounds like only one of us won at a tournament.

Neighborhood Boy #6

y favorite neighborhood boy came by on his bike. I saw him circling around the street looking for a conversation, and then he saw me on my porch and pulled up.

First, he wanted to do something I've started to call checking my bona fides. I don't know what he will do when he grows up, but he's seriously into data. It's like when you call the bank, and they ask you five questions to make sure it's you.

Tom, how old are you?

Fifty-two.

How old is Hugo?

Four and a half.

Skinny?

Six.

How many kids do you have?

One.

How old?

My daughter is fifteen.

Then he stops suddenly and, straddling his bike with his feet on the ground, he looks back down the street and then toward me again.

My great-grandmother died.

Oh, I'm sorry, buddy. That just happened?

No, it was a while ago. She was really old. Like a hundred forty.

Wow, yeah, that is old.

She's in heaven now. Do you know where heaven is?

Do you know where heaven is? I said.

He pointed up at a cloud formation. Up there, I think.

I nodded. Makes sense.

His voice got smaller. His small face crinkled as he asked me: Do you believe in heaven?

Now, there was no way I was about to have a theological discussion with a seven-year-old who was not my child. There was no way I was going to tell him the truth, that I was raised Catholic but pretty much became an atheist by the time I was sixteen. That before my confirmation, the priests pulled me into the rectory to interrogate me because I told one of them I didn't believe in God. They wanted me to recant, but I refused, the doubting Thomas to the end, and they confirmed me anyway, like how public schools move a second grader into third even if they can't do the work. No one wanted the hassle.

I believe in love, buddy, I said. You know if people love and don't hate, I think you can even have heaven here.

I saw him taking this in. He said, you want to see me do a jump?

Totally. Yeah, I want to see you do a jump.

Vaccine

o, after I got my first shot yesterday, I left the busy pharmacy and I had a banal errand to do, dog and cat food, and a short ride to the place, and on the way, suddenly, alone in my car, I wept.

This isn't so unusual for me—I've always been a soft touch. I used to choke up public speaking sometimes and need a minute. I also cry at the obvious places in movies, where they manipulate you with the swelling of the music.

This was more catharsis crying. Relief. A recognition of what a year it's been. More than five hundred thousand lost, including my sister's mother-in -law, and my sister-in-law's father. A partner of one of my siblings with long haul symptoms. Colleagues in academia and literary circles no longer here. An awareness, too, of my privilege. I stayed healthy, and sacrificed to do so, but it was easier for me than it was for so many others. A gratitude that my parents, my siblings, my ex-wife, and most of all my daughter have been safe. An anger at the time that has been lost, what a thief it is, and how it didn't really have to be this way. A mad respect for the brilliant people who created this liquid that went painlessly into my arm and is essentially a cure.

I thought about something a friend said that we should stop trying to return to normal. I think she's right. Normal, the previous normal, never worked for lots and lots of people. We should return to better. I'm an optimist, you know. I think we're headed there. One shot at a time. A recognition that we are one people. Progress is never a straight line. But there's lots of reason for hope. The snow is gone, rivers are running high, spring is here. I bought cat and dog food. I wore a mask. But I was a lot less afraid.

The Flower King

My parents are ninety years old. My mom almost, I should say. They live independently. They've been married for sixty-four years. They are now, thankfully, fully vaccinated. They're healthy. For the past year, one of my brothers and my sister-in-law, who live about a half hour away in Massachusetts, have done all their food shopping. They've barely left the fifty-five and up condo community they live in.

Tonight, I was on the phone with my mom when my dad came into the house. He was unaware she was on the phone.

The flower king is back, he announced loudly.

My mom said, oh.

I said, what's happening there?

She said, when your father and I were first dating, all my friends called him the flower king because he always brought me flowers. He's standing here now with a bouquet.

Where'd you go? My mother said to my dad while I was still on the phone.

Whole Foods, he said.

What were you doing there?

Getting flowers, beautiful Italian olives, Manchego cheese, and some lovely bread.

I said to my mom, I'll leave you guys to it.

What Do You Know about Brendan Behan?

I had this pang tonight of missing cities. I remembered, suddenly, an evening several years ago visiting New York. It was summer, warm, in the mid-seventies, beautiful night, the streets teeming with people. I had dinner with a lady friend outside at a great hole-in-the-wall Italian place on Amsterdam on the Upper West Side. I'd had good meetings that day and was feeling brightly. The server sold us on this dish of Tuscan steak with white beans and tomatoes. It had been on the food channel, she said. It was beautiful and simple and redolent of garlic and rosemary. Afterwards, not wanting the night to end, we walked leisurely down the busy avenue and decided to find a place to have another drink. We wanted something quiet where we could talk. We found a narrow bar, mostly empty, called The Dead Poet.

This one, I said.

We went in and sat down at the wooden bar. The door was open to the night. We ordered. We talked. A few minutes later an older couple on their way out stopped and the guy in his sixties said to us, I don't mean anything by this, but you two are very pretty together. He wore a tweed coat and put his hand on my shoulder.

We both laughed and thanked him. We weren't a couple, though we had thought about it. And on this night, I was rather smitten with her.

On the wall behind me was a large poster with the faces of Irish writers. No names though, just photos. The bartender saw me looking at it.

If you can name them all, he said, drinks are on the house.

Okay, I said. And I named them.

When I finished, his eyes narrowed and he said, I can't tell if you're a cheat or not.

Why?

No one, he said with a brogue I hadn't noticed earlier, gets Brendan Behan. Yeats, Shaw? Beckett? Of course. Behan, no.

I told him then my brother had lived in Galway in college and had approached a bar one night and was about to walk in when the door swung open and a fight spilled out onto the sidewalk, a full-on Donnybrook, six men or so throwing haymakers, and a couple of them saying in thick Irish accents, what do you know about Brendan Behan?

And I told the bartender that if grown men were willing to fight about a playwright, I ought to know who he was, so I looked him up, and ever since, his wide map of Ireland-like face has been imprinted on my brain.

I got your tab, he said.

The Much-Loved Bunny Speech

hen my daughter was nine, we were sharing a pizza at a local restaurant when she asked me if I wanted to know her Christmas list.

Bring it on, I said.

Okay, she said, brightly, warming up to this idea. You ready?

Definitely.

The whole *Percy Jackson* series by Rick Riordan.

Okay, I think, that's easy. Books. I mean we're trying to grow readers.

I nod enthusiastically. Cool, I said. That sounds great.

Chuck Taylor sneakers, she said, black. High-tops. Because they're rad.

I like rad, I say, in a way that suggests it's probably a word I never use.

Oh, and a bunny.

What do you mean, a bunny?

Like I said, a bunny.

A rabbit?

She gives me that look that will portend the teenager she will become, the one who believes in an alternate universe where someone has stolen grown-ups' brains and not vice versa.

Yes, she says, a bunny rabbit. Okay?

I took a long sip of my wine. Why do you want a bunny?

Because I'm a vegan.

This was a bridge too far. I said, no you're not, you ate a cheeseburger yesterday. You're eating a pizza now. That's the very definition of not being a vegan.

She took a pull off the straw in her root beer. Looked up at me with those big blue-green eyes.

I'm an aspiring vegan, she said unironically. And then took a bite of her cheese pizza.

There are no aspiring vegans, I said. Only people who ask you if this is vegan at a party. But anyway, it doesn't matter, the type of bunny people keep as pets are not in danger of being eaten. You're not saving them.

My girl was undeterred. She leaned forward, her elbows on the table and stared me down. She started to name check. Lulu has a bunny, she said, Anya has a bunny, Sadie has a bunny, Zoe has a bunny…

I raised my hand. Okay.

Forcefully she said, Daddy, I need in on that bunny action!

I laughed; I couldn't help it.

Christmas came. She got the whole Percy Jackson series. Some totally rad Chuck Taylor high-tops. Other cool things. But no bunny.

She was pissed. So, she did what any great artist would do. She took that anger and disappointment and turned it into art. She wrote a graphic novel. Super dark one. Its title?

Santa's Life of Lies.

A Funny Thing Happened on the Road to Publication

So, in 2006, one year after the hardcover of my second novel, *I'll Never Be Long Gone*, was published, HarperCollins released the paperback. The novel is set in a small-town restaurant in Vermont, and tells the story of two brothers, their legacy, and their love for the same woman. Right before publication, as always happens, my publisher sent me a box of the books as my contract requires. They looked great. I was showing off one to a friend of mine and she was flipping through it and said, weird that the font changes.

I said, what? But before she could answer that, she said, oh, cool drawing of a horse.

Let me see, I said.

Thing is, there was no horse in my book, and of course no illustrations. But there it was, a pen and ink illustration of a horse taking up a full page.

It took a few minutes to figure out what had happened, but for some reason twelve pages of my novel had been replaced by twelve pages of the children's novel, *My Friend Flicka*.

And they were a critical twelve pages, that included a very important sexual tryst that was key to the whole book. And while I was fuming about the terrible mistake, it suddenly occurred to me that if twelve pages of *My Friend Flicka* were in my book, then didn't that mean that my twelve-page sex scene must have been in *My Friend Flicka*?

Romance Is a Gentleman

I've been writing today and thinking of romantic gestures, big and small. I peaked early. When I was thirteen, I was in love with a girl three years older than me, which might as well have been ten or twenty years at that age. I could barely look at her—it was like looking at the sun. That summer on Cape Cod, I found myself one day on the same beach with her. She was with a group of friends; I was with a group of boys. It was a bright windy day and the sea sparkled like knives. The surf was high. We boys were jostling at the edge of the water and out of the corner of my eye, I was watching her as she and a row of friends moved out into the ocean, leaping off their feet as successive waves crashed into them.

Then it happened. A wave hit her perfectly and took away her bikini top. It was like we all noticed it at once, her shrieking, covering herself, her friends looking around, the water bringing her top like a gift to where I stood with a group of boys. The boys were elated. We were about to have the top. But I grabbed it out of the water and ignored the shouts behind me. I swam it out to her and when I reached her, I looked away demurely and held it out like an offering.

She swiftly fastened it back on and said to me, Tommy Greene, you are a sweetheart. I didn't know she even knew my name. She kissed me on the forehead and it's the only time we ever spoke. I've been chasing that feeling ever since.

A Murder of Crows

On my morning walk in the woods, it was dark and gloomy and the rain, although warm, was falling hard. A half mile into the park, I could hear the murder of crows. Sounded like there were hundreds of them. The deeper I went, the louder they got, invisible, high up in the treetops, the cacophony of their voices oddly terrifying. As Hugo and I came up the slope of a hillside, I could tell we were getting closer to where they were. Their sound was almost percussive it was so loud. At the top of the hill, two women, not together, both with dogs, too, were ten feet or so apart on the trail, looking west toward the treetops and where the crows must be.

I said jokingly, don't worry, they're here for me.

One of the women said, I now know why they call them a murder.

The other said, seriously. I've never heard them like this.

I lifted my head to the treetops. Quiet, my little ones, I said loudly.

And they shut the fuck up. Like that. Suddenly the only noise was the patter of rain landing on dead leaves.

Both women looked at me.

I laughed awkwardly. That was something, I said. Total joke. Wow. Crazy, right?

They each slowly backed up. Called their dogs. Left me and Hugo alone under the silent canopy.

When We Were Pretty

The other day, I got a DM from an old friend, S, who wrote to tell me that she and her husband, T, would be a few miles from me where their daughter was playing a playoff field hockey game at a nearby high school. They live two hours south of me, but I haven't seen them in at least a decade.

Might I be around?

Absolutely, I said, surprising myself.

It would have been easy to say no. It was short notice. And the weather was raw and shitty. Hard cold late fall rain. Like Wales in winter.

In years past, I may have come up with an excuse. And maybe it's the pandemic, or my own emerging sense of wanting to be present. To give into things. In truth, you might say we don't know each other well. We only spent two years at boarding school together in the late 1980s.

Since then, we've seen each other a few times. Though you could also say, perhaps, that we knew each other before we hardened into what we become, the layers of onion we all add as we age.

S was my first girlfriend at boarding school. A month after I arrived there, a fish out of water, the new kid, and she asked a mutual friend to invite me to a party at a faculty brat's house. Someone ate a goldfish. I knew she liked me. She was adorable, with wispy blond hair and green eyes. Dimpled cheeks. I had the courage to talk to her, and after that, we were into it, and at night, I was a boy with a girl and instead of going to the student union after study hall I would walk to her dorm and wait for her and we'd go to the soccer field and under the broad arch of the milky way, we would sit and stare at the stars and kiss. I would take off my tweed coat and lay it on the dewy ground, a gesture of a gentleman, and sometimes we'd sit like we were sledding on a toboggan, her in front of me, me behind her, my hands around her, my head nestled into her neck, practicing the language of love. Under that grand sky we thought we'd live forever.

T lived down the hall from me. We all looked up to him. He was red-headed and from Vermont, a place that felt foreign to me then. He played guitar, read literature as a hobby, and as a teenager had a wise gravitas that we all admired. We became fast friends.

A few months after we got together back then, S broke my heart. Dumped. I was devastated. I tried to be cold to her, walk past her like I didn't know who she was, but in a school like ours, it was too small. You couldn't do it. Shortly, she started dating a different close friend of mine, not T, and the two of us became friends again. It was a great life lesson for me, that hurt goes away, and sometimes relationships evolve and become something else, something better.

After high school, we all drifted apart. Different colleges. We saw each other a few times and then not at all. On 9/11, one of our friends died—he was high up in one of the towers—and I published a story about him, and S and others, seeing it, knew how to reach me, and got back in touch. We spent a weekend in southern Vermont pouring some on the ground for him, and I learned S and T were married, which blew me away and filled me with wonder. They found each other long after high school, fell in love, had three children, and built a life together.

The other afternoon, the three of us stood in a dismal rain and watched their daughter, who I had met briefly when she was a baby, now on the cusp of college, play her final field hockey game. The rain was icy cold. But it didn't matter. We let the unrelenting rain fall on us and told stories about when we were pretty.

We reminisced about one Easter. We were seventeen. We rode the train to S's mother's house in New Haven, a group of us. Easter morning her mother made us daiquiris, which stunned me, because it never would have happened at my house, and we ate brunch and got day-drunk and played croquet on a stretch of lawn next to a stucco house and laughed and danced with each other.

When we got on the train to go back to school, out the windows it was becoming spring. I remember feeling so grown up. Illicitly flush with alcohol, the Connecticut landscape passing by, in love with my friends, our youth, the possibilities that stretched out in front of us.

It's still there, right? Tell me. Even with the crow's feet radiating off our eyes and the grizzle of winter in my beard. It's still there.

Our Girl Jane

Jane died in Boston. She spent the first five months of her life at Dartmouth Hitchcock Medical Center in Hanover, New Hampshire, and the last month at Boston Children's Hospital. The only time she had been outside a hospital in her whole life was the ambulance ride between the two.

Though if you were to look at her, outside of the omnipresent tubes that helped her breathe, Jane was a beautiful baby. Born so tiny, she had gotten fat on breast milk. Her chin had a roll or two. Her full head of hair, dark brown, would lighten, we thought, and eventually be blonde, like her sister. But her eyes were this rich, knowing brown unlike her blue-eyed older sister.

I was at the college when I got the call. January. Bright sun off the snow. Cold but a clear blue day.

She's not going to make it. If you want to say goodbye,

you need to come now.

I was in front of College Hall. The fountain, turned off for the season, was in front of me. I lit a cigarette and looked out across the expanse of snow-covered green. I knew I should be all motion, a rush of activity, calling my assistant, letting her know, a race to Boston in my car.

But I stood there for the length of a cigarette, hating myself for it, but also letting the last six months move through me. The highs, we were so close to coming home, the strange normalcy of the NICU when you've been there long enough, the reason people often compare it to combat: long stretches of boredom suddenly punctuated by moments of extreme terror. The funny thing is that we don't know our capacity until we're asked to use it. It's always greater than we think. Jane taught me that; this pandemic continues to teach me that.

I swung by my house and stuffed a bag with clothes and then got on the road. I drove insanely fast—I had in the back of my mind a fantasy of getting stopped by the cops and explaining why I was lighting up the highway. It distracted me, the righteousness of this idea, being able to say in response to the query, is there an emergency?

Yeah, my daughter is dying.

Oh, follow us, sir. We will get you there.

Lights flash and we move together like an army.

Before Jane {okay this hasn't changed much}, I had always been terrified of medical shit. Then I found myself living part time in a hospital. We knew we were facing a marathon, not a sprint. My wife and I did shifts. I'd often go down in the afternoon and stay into the evening. Just Jane and I and her nurses. Since Jane's issues were her lungs, I crammed on all things related to respiratory therapy. It felt like the only thing I could contribute—to learn as much as possible. One time a new doctor came on. While they were doing their rounds, they were talking about settings for nitric oxide, which Jane was on.

I piped up. You know there is some interesting new research on weaning off it that just came out.

The doctor in charge said to me, dismissively, where did you hear that? Dr. Google?

Actually, no, I said. This month's *New England Journal of Medicine*. It just came out; I'm not surprised you haven't seen it yet. I read it last night.

Several months in, I was running the weekly doctor's meetings when it came to Jane's care. It happened organically, part of it me being used to running things, part of it was how unusual our length of stay was, part of it was the structure of the hospital where doctors went on weeks-long shifts before disappearing for months. We were the constants.

One day we were all meeting in a conference room off the NICU. Jane's amazing nurses, respiratory therapists, the residents, and the doctor on duty. The fragile two of us. I was presiding at the head of the table, when Dr. Little, the renowned doctor who first saw Jane after her birth and had said, looking at her in her bubble, legs kicking, I'll say this much, I like her spirit, opened the door, and walked in. We hadn't seen him in months.

He was in his seventies and had founded this NICU some thirty-plus years before. He saw me leading the meeting and was flabbergasted. He motioned to me and said, can I see you outside for a moment?

I followed him into the hallway. We walked in silence. When we came to the door that led out of the NICU and to the rest of the hospital, we stopped. Dr. Little turned toward me. He was tall and slender, bald with a gray goatee. I was against the wall, and he was in front of me.

Let me be honest, he said. When I walked in there today and saw a parent running the meeting, I was pissed. It felt like a breakdown of norms. But then I put myself in your shoes and you know what? I probably would have done the same thing. I admire you, friend. You know how I don't shake hands?

I did. I remembered this. He always simulated shaking hands from a foot or so away, not willing to risk bringing anything to the tiny babies he treated every day. I nodded. Yes, I know.

Dr. Little stuck his hand out. Well, I want to shake your hand. As a dad, myself.

We shook hands. Looked into each other's eyes. Firm. Our hands clasped together for what felt like a long time. Two willful men of different generations. Strangers sharing a moment as intimate as almost anything in my life. I thought I might cry but I didn't.

I remembered moments like this on my way down to Boston to steel myself against the truth that this road was coming to an end, and now. And here's the thing about moments like this: you drive. You do the task at hand. You do the only thing you're required to. You show up.

And that's the thing about resilience: we're all stronger than we think we are.

I parked in the parking garage and raced into the building; took the elevator to the sixth floor. Half-ran by the nurse's station and when I came to Jane's bed, she was in her mother's arms, her aunt and uncle there, too, but something was different. She was untethered. No tubes leading out of her throat, no tubes leading out of the PICC line in her chest. No IVs. She looked like any other baby, but she was dying, and you could tell by the oxygen numbers from the last thing connected to her. They had sunk fast.

In the sixties when we all want to be above ninety-five. During this journey, joyous nights, and days for us had been when Jane was doing what they called "high-satting." The machine would hit 100, like pinball, and it made a sound over and over. One of the few happy sounds of the NICU.

This is how most of us will die when it's our time. The oxygen will leave our bodies. Jane had spent her whole life trying to keep it in, and she didn't want to anymore.

A month or so earlier, back on the nights when it was my shift to be with her, they would dim the lights in her little corner of the NICU at Dartmouth, and I would read to her while she slept next to me in her crib. I read for her and inadvertently, for the other babies near her. I read her the same stuff I used to read to Sarah, books that had that resonance of tone, the incantation where the words and the story came together. *Strega Nona.*

Jane could never tell me what she thought about this. I didn't know if she liked it, or was indifferent, or if it helped anyone but me.

But coming into the hospital on her last day, rising above the cacophony of sound, to Jane, was my voice suddenly loud and frantic. And while her mother held her, something remarkable happened. Jane's oxygen spiked when she heard me. For a moment she went back to a 100.

Because of the sound of a father. Her eyes opened a little, so lovely and brown, and it was fleeting but it broke my heart. The sentience of it, how much more a baby knows than we think they should.

I couldn't watch her die. My wife understood this about me, but it didn't make me feel less like a coward. I held her for a moment, and I broke inside and couldn't stop crying. I kissed her forehead and I handed her back to Tia. I said goodbye. I careened back out the way I came, out the long hallway, the cavernous elevators, the lobby, through the revolving doors and out into the winter day which had turned gray here in the city.

I was gasping for breath. I sat down on this stone wall, the building rising high behind me. Traffic in front of me, ambulances, cabs, the relentlessness of a downtown hospital. All around me the buildings were close. A large extended family came out of the revolving doors, a boy maybe six or seven in the middle of the scrum holding a bunch of balloons so big it looked like it could sweep him up in the air and into the sky.

They were celebrating. He was going home—from what horror, he survived, I will never know. Their joy was a joy I guess I had imagined and one that would never become true for us. We weren't all going home.

They stopped in front of me. And maybe it was because I

was alone, and looked respectable, still in my college tweed and dark jeans and wingtips, that a woman said to me, motioning to her camera, would you mind?

They didn't see the redness in my eyes.

I stood up and took their photo, my grief hidden like an ancient family secret. A reminder that the world keeps moving like those revolving doors.

It wasn't until they left that I cried again and then it wouldn't stop.

A day later, we returned to Vermont. The college campus, when I walked on it, was covered everywhere in hearts. Every door, many of the windows. Students were asking why. The president lost his daughter, they were told. A faculty member I had often battled with stopped me in a hallway and looked deeply into my eyes and said, I hold you in the light, and I could tell she meant it. Across the street from our house were luminaries that spelled Jane Was Here.

These last words came from the final blog post my wife did about Jane. When Jane was born, Tia began writing a blog to keep our close family and friends informed, since it was too much to talk on the phone with everyone every single day, and this thing was going to be a roller coaster. But a funny thing happened. Tia was a terrific writer, and she wrote less about the struggle of Jane, and more the life of Jane. Her posts were funny. She called each nurse Awesome nurse (first initial of their name) and gave the doctors nicknames. She wrote with a wry sense of humor of life in the NICU. At the end of Jane's life, she had six thousand daily readers, a number I and most of my novelist friends would have killed for.

After Jane died, Tia wrote one last post. She asked her readers to send a postcard from wherever they were that said, Jane was here. It was from the Dr. Suess story, *Horton Hears a Who*, and the idea that a person is a person no matter how small. We are here! The Who's shout. She gave our address.

And the postcards started to come. From all over the country. Hundreds a day. And not only postcards—but art, drawings, quilts, photos of the words Jane was here drawn in the sand. The poet Mary Ruefle, I remember, sent an elaborate set of handmade cards with tiny poems on them.

At the end of a month, postcards came from all fifty states. We had a map with pins in it. They came from all over the world, too, most of the countries in Europe. And after about eight months, we had cards from six of the seven continents, the only one of course we didn't have was Antarctica.

It was a remarkable tribute to the power of the beautiful, brown-eyed baby girl fighting for her life. But it wasn't over, yet.

A year after Jane died, a final postcard came to our door. It was from Antarctica. Scientists at the station there, outside in subfreezing temperatures, dark-green coats with fur-lined hoods, holding a sign in their collective arms.

Jane was here.

Neglected Gardens #2

laine, the woman who once owned my house and asked me if she could garden here again, and to bring back the gardens that were once her life's work, comes here every day when the weather is good. Delta is the new variant, but the pandemic still feels like it's receding. It's summer in Vermont and the days are long and pretty. I've been spending more time in town these days, and less at the lake, which means we are often here at the same time. It's nice. We've become friends. She gardens in the yard in front of me, while I write on the porch.

I admire her work ethic. When she's going, she doesn't care if it's dumping rain. She unloads trunk loads of rocks out of her trunk that she brings here from somewhere else and arranges in the dirt. She has new plants and bark to lay down. She wears her Texas Longhorn's baseball hat.

Sometimes she wants my opinion on something, it is my house after all, but I usually listen intently and then say what I said when we first met.

This is your canvas. Do what you would do if you still lived here.

You sure it's not weird?

It's only weird if we make it weird.

Right, she said.

Mostly, on those summer days the two of us worked in silence, though sometimes we talked. I told her about the novel I was working on; she told me about writing her dissertation in this house. She had been an elementary school principal before she retired. We talked about my daughter, her daughter, her grandchildren. Now and again, she would find a plant or a small tree and contemplate it, wonder if she was the one who planted it before invariably determining that she had. *Thirty years ago.*

Once, she told me her husband would not drive down this street. Even though they lived two blocks away. That he had not seen this house since they moved out some eight years ago after being here for twenty-eight. He can't do it, she said. We bought this place when we first got together.

She looked away wistfully. We had a great life here. I wish you could have seen the basement.

The basement is finished here, which is incredibly

unusual in this neighborhood of all old Victorians. Most of them have narrow ceilings and earthen floors. Mine has a bar, a bathroom, a small fridge. I have it set up as a gym that I never use.

My husband is Scottish, she said. He played professional soccer. He loves soccer and pubs. He had small tables down there, a television that showed the European games and posters. It was his sanctuary. His friends would come over and he would serve them beers from behind the bar. We were both sad to leave but it made sense. It was too much house.

I thought about this. All my life I had been restless. Moving often. I'm not that old and I've owned a lot of different houses. I've never gotten attached to places, though a possible exception is my lake cabin. There is a magic there for me. As for this house, I bought it because it was around the corner from my wife and daughter after we split. I bought nice furniture, hung some art. Redid the kitchen. But it never felt like a home to me. Before Covid-19, I basically just slept here.

The summer moved on. A beautiful late July day. Elaine was working on this rock garden right in front of my porch. She was laboring over a big stone that once it was settled would look like a shark fin coming out of the ground.

I have two porches here. One off my kitchen that I write

on at a table. And a second one in front of the house that I don't really use. The mail goes there. I can see a slice of it from where I sit.

Suddenly, I heard Elaine turn her head and say, oh, hey, honey.

And I looked up and there was a man, clean-shaven, handsome, around seventy, sitting on the front steps some twenty feet away from us.

I brought your lunch, he said to his wife. She beamed but away from him, where he couldn't see it. Back digging like it couldn't wait.

David, she said, without looking up, this is Tom.

I'm glad you're here, David, I said.

He nodded. Thank you.

I thought about asking him if he wanted to come inside and look around, but I could tell it was too soon. He looked like a man in a dentist's waiting room. In the two of them I saw suddenly the history they had here, the formative years of their life, the joy, of course, but also the recognition that time goes by in a flash. We can do our best to slow it, but it's not easy. Time is the greatest thief of all.

But it's not true when they say that you can't go back home again. But when you do, you might need to ease your way in the door.

The End

About the Author

Pandemic selfie courtesy of the author

Thomas Christopher Greene is the author of six novels, including the international bestseller *The Headmaster's Wife*. His fiction has been translated into thirteen languages. Tom is also the founder of the Vermont College of Fine Arts where he served as president for thirteen years. He makes his home in Montpelier, Vermont.

 **More Nonfiction from Rootstock Publishing:**

A Peek Under the Hood: Heroin, Hope, & Operation Tune-Up
  by Michael Pevarnik
A Judge's Odyssey by Dean B. Pineles
A Lawyer's Life to Live by Kimberly B. Cheney
Alzheimer's Canyon: One Couple's Reflections on Living with Dementia
  by Jane Dwinell & Sky Yardley
Attic of Dreams: A Memoir by Marilyn Webb Neagley
Catalysts for Change ed. by Doug Wilhelm
China in Another Time by Claire Malcolm Lintilhac
Circle of Sawdust: A Circus Memoir of Mud, Myth, Mirth, Mayhem and Magic
  by Rob Mermin
Collecting Courage: Anti-Black Racism in the Charitable Sector
  eds. Nneka Allen, Camila Vital Nunes Pereira, & Nicole Salmon
Cracked: My Life After a Skull Fracture by Jim Barry
I Could Hardly Keep From Laughing by Don Hooper & Bill Mares
Nobody Hitchhikes Anymore by Ed Griffin-Nolan
Pauli Murray's Revolutionary Life by Simki Kuznick
Preaching Happiness by Ginny Sassaman
Red Scare in the Green Mountains by Rick Winston
Save Me a Seat! A Life with Movies by Rick Winston
Striding Rough Ice: Coaching College Hockey and Growing Up In the Game
  by Gary Wright
Tales of Bialystok: A Jewish Journey from Czarist Russia
  by Charles Zachariah Goldberg
The Atomic Bomb on My Back by Taniguchi Sumiteru
The Language of Liberty by Edwin C. Hagenstein
The Last Garden by Liza Ketchum
The Morse Code: Legacy of a Vermont Sportswriter by Brendan Buckley
Uncertain Fruit: A Memoir of Infertility, Loss, and Love
  by Rebecca & Sallyann Majoya
Walking Home: Trail Stories by Celia Ryker
You Have a Hammer: Building Grant Proposals for Social Change
  by Barbara Floersch

Learn about our Fiction, Poetry, and Children's titles at
www.rootstockpublishing.com.